Momer

Kimberly Bond

BookLeaf Publishing
India | USA | UK

Moments in Verse © 2023 Kimberly Bond

All rights reserved.

No part of this publication may be reproduced, stored in a retrieval system, or transmitted, in any form or by any means, electronic, mechanical, photocopying, recording or otherwise, without the prior written permission of the presenters.

Kimberly Bond asserts the moral right to be identified as the author of this work.

Presentation by *BookLeaf Publishing*

Web: www.bookleafpub.com

E-mail: info@bookleafpub.com

ISBN: 9789358313925

First edition 2023

To my parents and grandparents who always had an unwavering belief that I was meant to be a writer.

To Mr Patterson, for those last words I will never forget.

To my brother and sister, who always encourage me to be 'me'.

ACKNOWLEDGEMENT

Thanks to everyone who has supported me, inspired me, encouraged me to write, to innovate, to use words to make change happen. Thank you to my amazing husband who encouraged me to take part in this writing challenge and publish this book. I love you. Thank you to my wonderful friends who 'get' me and appreciate my weirdness and understand some of my inspiration.

No Seeing

All my nerves are gone,
My soul is disappearing,
All I've seen is slipping through my fingers.

To hear the rushing of the water,
To hear laughter, when I laugh no more
is like torture
because my soul is disappearing.

Everything is black,
because light is what I lack.
My feelings are damp,
no light from the lamp
because my soul is disappearing.

Only hearing, never seeing,
to hear the sound of people
crying, laughing, what I do no more
is like torture
because my soul is disappearing
because I am blind.

A day in the life of my clowder

Through the bushes I prowl,
Unseen and mysterious,
A creature in the night,

Through the grass I tiptoe,
on my soft delicate socks,
In the corner I curl,
with my thick grey tail,
wrapped around me,

I watch the moon looking over me,
as I wash my dark ears
and then sleep
until morning,
when I will awaken as the sun rises
over my territory
and run!
run with the wind!
beginning my hunt for the tastiest morsel

of feral delight
and I will meet with my clowder,
and discuss worldly things
until the moon bears down upon us once more.

Snow day

The snow is here,
everything is white;
Let's go and have
a snowball fight.

Let's go outside
and wrap up warm;
Let's run in a frenzy
in the midst of a snowstorm.

Let's throw snowballs,
let's do a twirl;
Let's make snow angels
and watch the snow whirl.

It's getting dark,
let's go inside,
sit by the fire
and curl up tight.

The snow has melted,
it's gone away;
Let's hope it will be back
another day.

Ode to the Christmas Tree

There you sit
proud and tall
like a god
looking down upon his worshippers
and how we laugh
and stare in delight
as we adorn you with gifts that shine and flash
and hang on your many arms.

There you sit
as we drink in your piney aroma
and you look down upon us
unaware your worshippers
will soon turn away
and you will be stripped and torn apart
and then you will be thrown

in the deepest, darkest pit
and your life will be over.

New Year

Time has passed,
but we breathe in
everything new;
the sun
more gentle,
smiles wider,
sentiments sweeter,

Everything glows
basks in this new light
spreads the message of hope
brings focus to the future,

Everyone sees it
feels it in their heart
the worries of yesteryear
exactly that -
gone -

with the puff of midnight,

The clock ticks,
starts over,
Happy New Year!

The Crystal Mistress

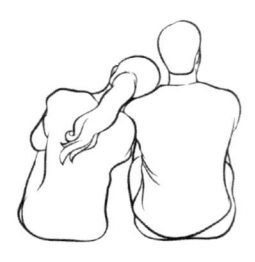

Her mind, ever overwhelming
bubbles and ticks, full of questions;
the who's and what's and why's of everyday life.
The smiles she has to fake
and the layer of doubt underneath
makes her forget what her heart truly desires-
to be free as a bird,
to laugh and to love,
to forget about the ticking clocks
and the endless to-do lists that surround her life
like the barricades on a castle wall.

And so she sits here,
with the crystal mistress
and wonders what it would be like
to forget.
The voice it beckons, a cool whisper in the night
air,
and she swallows
and oh - what's this?

the night shadows become wonderful moving objects;
lampposts become men, laughing, talking in the dead of night.
The moon it shines like the light of an angel
And then she sees him.
The One, who makes her forget the time and the ticking clocks and the endless to-do lists that surround her life.
Instead she sits, admires the light in his eyes, the mischief in his smile
the soft skin of his hands and oh! the gentle touch of his lips on hers.
He who pours the flame of light into her heart and her eyes are only for him tonight.
She is as free as a bird,
finally she can rise up and be who she is meant to be;
the confidante, the lover, the cruel mistress, the damsel in distress!

Soon, she knows she will go back
to the ticking clocks and the endless to-do lists,
but now she sits and holds him close,
their heartbeats entwined.
Euphoria.

Lover's Hands

A touch of your hand,
a wink of your eye;
is this flirting? you say
oh my! Oh my!

A stroke of your hand,
a kiss of your lips;
A touch of your nipples
and writhe of your hips.

A dance of your fingers
as they move inside me,
feelings rise up and up
like the waves of the sea.

A clasp of your hand
as I pull you in close,
Lay my head on your bosom,
this is what I love the most.

Airport conversations

Here we sit, side by side,
our lives entwined in this brief moment
through the choice of the same destination.
Here we sit, patiently waiting
all in our own world
each on a different journey, our own unique
flight.

Here we sit, our minds racing
as we share a small slice of our lives;
stories of work and children,
houses and cars
holidays and funerals
loved ones past and present
laughter and grief,
all in that same brief moment.

Here we sit,
we have reached our destination,

created a flicker of connection
and now we continue our journey onwards
Our hearts carrying the echoes of this shared moment,
bound by the threads of time.

The Tortoise and the Mouse

The legend of the giant Tortoise,
who had a house on the back of his shell,
begins with a little mouse,
whose name was Caramel.

For little Caramel needed a ride,
and somewhere safe that he could hide.
So when he saw the Tortoise,
he stopped and asked for a lift,
"Sure!" said the Tortoise,
"Consider this a gift."

So Caramel took his worldly belongings,
and put them in a sack,
and then he built a little house,
On top of Tortoise's back.

Word soon spread far and wide,
about the tortoise and the mouse,
When other animals came to look,

They marvelled at the house.

Then others clambered aboard,
The house on Tortoise's back,
Rats and hamsters and guinea pigs too,
Everyone was part of the pack.

With every new animal,
the house got bigger and bigger,
and so this story was repeated,
each time with a little more vigour.

It is said the giant Tortoise,
Who had a house on the back of his shell,
Loved and cared for his friends,
But especially little Caramel.

And so the legend doesn't yet have an ending,
Or at least not one that is known.
Perhaps the pair are still out there,
Wandering, but never alone.

The Lover's Debt

The hooded figure loomed over him,
Easily two meters tall,
But when he turned and faced it,
He wasn't scared at all.

For under the hood,
Stood a beautiful young man,
Whose eyes were bright and blue.
"Hello," he said with a smile on his face,
"What can I do for you?"

"I'm here to collect my debt," the figure said,
"You need to pay me what you owe.
It may seem like it's too soon,
But you have to reap what you sow."

The words filled him with a sense of dread,
Because not a penny did he have.
So instead he took his sword,

And let it feel his wrath.

Slash! The figure's head was on the floor,
Beautiful blue eyes and all.
But little did he know,
It was the man he did adore.
For clasped in the figure's hand,
Was the most beautiful ring;
Now never destined to be on his finger,
But simply the source of his heart's sting.

Under the Sakura Tree

The young girl sits
Under the Sakura tree.
Is this it? She wonders,
Is this all that life is meant to be?

For her life has been fleeting,
Like the day the blossom blooms,
Full of moments of beauty,
And others of doom and gloom.

But in fleeting days, there are times embrace,
A second's whisper, a lifetime's trace.
Years dance by, like leaves in the wind,
Moments cherished, memories pinned.

And so here she sits, on the mountain's edge,
The world below, so picturesque.
Life and love, land and sea,
Her soul the only connection
To fragile mortality.

For in this place,
Where mountains meet,
And Sakura's embrace is so sweet,
She learns the essence of it all,
That life is but a fleeting thrall.

Beneath the petals that fall,
Like dreams set free,
She is finally at peace,
Under the Sakura tree.

Lockdown Reflections

When we look back now,
It all seems a bit strange,
Locked in our homes,
Like wild animals with mange.

"You must stay at home!"
Said Boris on the TV,
But then went and partied in his garden,
Rubbing his hands with glee.

The stats told us people were dying,
The graphs getting ever bigger,
All while the Tories were lying,
behind our backs with a snigger.

For what it's worth,
The weather was great,
But that was perhaps
the only saving grace.

No sunshine could make up for
The months away from family,
No touching, no hugging,
2m apart, no room to get comfy.

The virus was real,
The country in collective shock,
Now we're all angry,
we were being mocked.

We spent two years,
Not seeing smiles,
Our only socials,
Meeting down the shopping aisles.

We can look back now,
And it all seems a blur,
But I think we can
all concur;
we'll be telling future generations
What went on
Unprecedented! never seen before!
And 3 years later it's still not gone...

But then lockdown did
change some things for the better,
The power of community,
It really did matter;

Those that stepped up,
did so with love,
Friendships and connections made,
And collectively we got tough

Behind the mask

Step outside,
The world anew
A tapestry of faces
With masks we can't undo.

Behind each mask a silent tale
Of strength and hope that will not fail
Concealing fears, yet our eyes betray
We all yearn for a brighter day.

For when we have masks adorned
A symbol of a world transformed
A shield to guard, keep at bay
The unseen foe that sought to sway.

Eyes meet eyes, but lips are mute
Expressions lost, a subtle brute
Faces hidden, smiles concealed
The warmth of kinship seems repealed.

For though the masks may cause a divide
They also serve as ties that bind
Let us not forget this hour
When masks became a source of power.

Now the world emerges new
And masks no longer hide our view.
We cherish lessons learned so well
And in our hearts, the stories tell.

Autumn Leaves

Whispers of autumn leaves in the wind
A tale of seasons;
beginnings end and ends begin.
They dance and they flutter,
As they begin to fall,
away from their homes of trees so tall.

Shades of gold and crimson,
a delightful hue
As they fade, they make way for the new.

They carpet the earth in a quilt of their own,
a tapestry woven in colours full-blown,
they cradle the whispers of days gone by,
As autumn's caress bids summer goodbye.

Alexander the Cat

Alexander the cat or
Dinkle-Puss the Third
Was the proud owner of a hat
that was very absurd

For the hat atop his regal head
It did sit askew
With feathers and buttons affixed
On top of a bright cobalt blue

He was a feline of flair
A princely display
His hat catching moonbeams in a most
wonderous display

He'd strut through the garden
Like a grand feline ballet
In the meadow He'd frolic
Come night or day

For under the hat
Was a magical world
Where dreams and adventures
They did unfurl

Alexander the cat, so sly and wise
With wonder gleaming in his eyes
Navigated this mystical place
With both elegance and grace

Each step a dance, each turn a twirl
In his whimsical, enchanted world
Through fields of emerald and meadows of lace
He'd roam with a quiet, measured pace

And as the sun would start to wane
And evening's shadows stretched and gained
He'd bid farewell to this hidden sphere

He'd return to his garden
To prance and gambol, so gallant and bold
With his hat as a banner
A story to be told.

Rainy day reflections

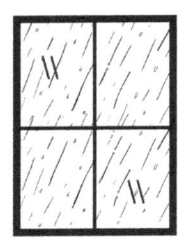

Why must
Raindrops
Adorn my windows
And angry clouds
Fill the sky?
When all I want, all we need
Is the comforting warmth of sunshine
Like the touch of a friend's hand on your back
Gently encouraging you forward.
Maybe there will be a rainbow,
To bring back the hope of better days,
Through the gloom,
Of the pitter patter raindrops,
On my window.

Just for one night

It was just for one night;
she wanders with a confident swagger down a
side street
as the sun starts to set.

It's just for one night, she reassures herself
as she pulls a jacket over her shoulders and
approaches one of the local beggars
she often sees out by Greggs in the morning.

It's just for one night;
this is what she says to the man
who stops on the street corner
as she holds out her thumb to passing cars

It's just for one night, she mutters to herself once
again
as she lays on the bed and
lets the man touch her
move inside her,

and later hand her a hundred pounds
and leaves her once again on the street corner.

It was always just for one night
her best friend Margaret tells the solemn audience
at her funeral twelve months later.
It's just that for some people, that night never ends.

Love Haiku

Your smile makes me smile,
my heart gives everything
away to you.

Whispers of wilted Love

You my love,
A product of my yearning heart,
Burdened by unspoken words
I dare not lay bare.

For the echoes of our passion,
Always in my mind
The caress of your fingers
Forever on rewind.

The sound of your laughter,
Your soft cherry lips,
Memories of your kisses,
And the trace of your hips.

Our love, it is one that was rare
But like wilted petals,
love's bloom is unfair

Now that love's Ember fades
A solitary flare
Unseen, unheard,
my heart's lonely prayer.

Home Office

Home. Home Office,
Home should be where the heart is
and if it's in England that's okay
but thousands live in fear
the Home Office might take it all away.

Home. Office
purveyors of hostile policy
hosts of fear and stress
when all these poor families want to do
is settle down and worry less.

Home. Office.
the words of hypocrisy
a place you think would be welcoming,
a safe haven for those who have made journeys
we can't imagine,

not here for holiday or pleasure
and they certainly didn't arrive at their leisure
when bombs have fallen on the homes
that they have always known.

Home. Office.
In shadows cast by policies,
Lies fear, like a shroud,
Families seeking refuge,
Yet met with a hostile crowd.

Their stories etched in every line,
Of struggles faced and battles won,
Yet met with scepticism and doubt,
Their journey far from done.

Oh, Home. Office,
Your doors should open wide,
To those in need of shelter,
From lands where they can't abide.

Let compassion be your guiding star,
Replace hostility with care,
For in the end, we're all but travellers,
Seeking solace, love, and a place to share.

Bella the Cat

In a world of whiskers, soft and fine
there dances a feline, graceful, divine.
Her name is Bella, a regal sight
She has eyes that gleam like a moonlit night.

Bella, oh Bella, with your whiskers aglow
in gardens you wander, to and fro
You chase the butterflies, light as air
A ballet of beauty, beyond compare.

You perch on a windowsill
eyes wide and bright
gazing at stars that adorn the night.

With a purr that hums like a gentle stream
you curl up next to me, as if in a dream
with the warmth of a blanket's tender embrace
you find your solace
your sacred space.